LINCOLN CHRISTIAN COLLEGE

O9-BTO-360

# Work as Praise

EDITORS

*George W. Forell*

*William H. Lazareth*

JUSTICE

BOOKS

FORTRESS PRESS      PHILADELPHIA

Biblical quotations from the Revised Standard Version of the Bible, copyrighted 1946, 1952, © 1971, 1973 by the Division of Christian Education of the National Council of the Churches of Christ in the U.S.A., are used by permission.

COPYRIGHT © 1979 BY FORTRESS PRESS

All rights reserved. No part of this publication may be reproduced, stored in a retrieval system, or transmitted in any form or by any means, electronic, mechanical, photocopying, recording, or otherwise, without the prior permission of the copyright owner.

**Library of Congress Cataloging in Publication Data**

Main entry under title:

Work as praise.

   (Justice books)
   Bibliography: p.
   1. Work (Theology)—Addresses, essays, lectures. 2. Vocational—Biblical teaching—Addresses, essays, lectures. 3. Manpower policy—United States—Moral and religious aspects—Addresses, essays, lectures. 4. Unemployed—United States—Moral and religious aspects—Addresses, essays, lectures. 5. Right to labor—Moral and religious aspects—Addresses, essays, lectures. I. Forell, George Wolfgang. II. Lazareth, William Henry, 1928–      III. Series.
BT738.5.W67    261.8'5    78-54549
ISBN 0-8006-1555-7

7119A79   Printed in the United States of America   1-1555

# Contents

64952

# Foreword

THIS issue of Justice Books is devoted to the challenge of chronic unemployment in our boom-and-bust economy. "In the beginning, God created . . ." (Gen. 1:1). Since persons are created in the image of this ever-creating God, work is a distinctive mark of our humanity. Therefore unemployment is at depth a moral issue that transcends the statistical fluctuations of our economic charts, tables, and trend analyses.

Richard H. Luecke first looks beneath the statistics and traces the accelerating growth of "labor" at the expense of "work." A historical review of the meaning of work in various cultures concludes by documenting the transformation and displacement of work in modern agriculture and manufacturing. Five criteria are proposed for policies and actions bearing on our present structural unemployment and the future of work.

Following Luecke's description of the ethical challenges of unemployment, George H. Brand annotates some recent studies that seek to humanize the work process and analyze the inflation-unemployment tradeoffs in economic policy.

Foster R. McCurley and John H. Reumann then deal with the theme of work in the providence of God. They review the ambivalent witness in the Scriptures to work, both as part of God's good creation and as painful toil because of human sin. The economic views of Jesus and Paul are evaluated in their original setting and for their value in Christian proclamation today.

"Work as Praise" is developed by William H. Lazareth as a theological response in Christian economic ethics. Affirming the church as the communion of saints, the Christian life-style of responsible freedom, and the calling of all baptized believers to serve as priests of God's saving gospel and prophets of God's righteous law, the author goes on to advocate the integral relation of one's Christian vocation to an economic occupation in the daily struggle for social justice.

George W. Forell concludes with some trenchant comments on the current state of the "Protestant work ethic" and the economic crisis of the Protestant clergy. Structural unemployment will soar unchallenged so long as acquisitive Americans go on believing and acting as if "God helps those who help themselves."

W.H.L.

# Unemployment and the Future of Work

## *Richard H. Luecke* *

### INTRODUCTION

ANY advocacy in matters of social welfare is less than sufficient today if it does not include economic policies and structures. For instance, advocacy for civil rights is less than helpful if it does not recognize how civil rights have become dependent on economic as well as social and cultural rights. No less a person than John C. Bennett, a well-known social justice advocate, has called for a "return to economic issues as having central importance for Christian ethics."

There are many avenues by which to approach the social welfare issues of our day, but none seems at once more personal and more public, more currently economic and more traditionally theological than the question of work—and worklessness.

During his candidacy President Carter called unemployment "the number one domestic issue for the next four to eight years." In his first State of the Union Message he reasserted that "the right to work for a decent living is one we cannot and will not ignore." After his meetings with other heads of state, headlines reported that these international leaders saw unemployment as

---

*The author has taught at Valparaiso University, Indiana, and is now a staff member of the Community Renewal Society in Chicago, Illinois.

"the number one issue." This problem has come to occupy center stage in most advanced industrial societies.

In the finer print, these leaders posed the problem as "unemployment and inflation" or "unemployment and youth." Our disposition to say "unemployment *and*"—unemployment *and* women, the aged, the family, the neighborhood, the city, welfare, mental health, energy, technology, to which we may add "faith and work"—shows how unemployment touches many other issues now deeply troubling us.

Fundamental inquiry must be done in situations where the way to greater understanding seems blocked. The problem of unemployment is one such situation. It becomes insufficient in this circumstance to speak simply of continued problem solving, if that is taken to mean the "problems" of unemployment are well defined and agreed upon and all we need to do is extend familiar "solutions." In that case, solutions may serve to define the problems rather than the other way around. In the matter of work today, we find ourselves dealing with "issues" rather than with "problems." Issues emerge when new data are no longer accommodated by previous conceptions, when we are no longer entirely sure what the problem really is or where the problem really lies. "The worst, most corrupting of lies," said Georges Bernanos, "is a problem poorly stated."

Issue airing, which is prior to problem solving, is a function of all citizens. It does not require, at least not initially, the work of technical specialists. It *does* require continued reference to fundamental human considerations alongside of new material and economic conditions.

Religious and ethical commitments serve to raise questions we might otherwise prefer to let lie and to sustain questions we might prefer to drop. Ethical conceptions enter into the formation of new judgments. Traditional themes help to mark out fresh lines of investigation and action. (Conversely, it is exactly through such discussion and action that basic convictions become activated, tested, and clarified.) Thus it is a function of the religious community not merely to support specific public proposals bearing on the present unemployment but to enrich the discussion that surrounds such proposals.

## LOOKING BENEATH THE STATISTICS

It is symptomatic of our inherited economic assumptions that we usually approach the question of unemployment in terms of a monthly figure designating "the total unemployed as percent of the civilian labor force." This percentage figure finds its way to news columns and broadcasts from data published by the Bureau of Labor Statistics on the basis of a telephone survey of 47,000 households for the twelfth day of each month. The unemployment figure serves as a "leading economic indicator" of business cycles and calls attention to shifts in forms of employment; it reveals "cyclical" and "frictional" unemployment which can be addressed by the "fine tuning" of monetary and tax measures. The figure also plays a role in assigning amounts of federal revenue sharing and in targeting government spending. But it does not help us much as we seek to understand the basic problem of unemployment.[1]

During recent years the percentage of those unemployed but actively seeking work has fluctuated at higher levels than at any time since the Great Depression of the 1930s. A crude breakdown of these figures reveals a percentage half again as high for blue-collar workers as for service personnel, almost 2½ times as high for black workers as for white, near 20 % for teenagers, and well over 40 % for black teenagers. But statistics like these which refer to everywhere in general do not describe any place in particular. They do not identify personal hardship or effects on family and social life. They do not touch such questions as the importance of work in the lives of young people or of aging workers who are pressed into early retirement. They do not count "discouraged workers" or the "handicapped" who have given up looking for jobs, nor do they take account of the "underemployment" of involuntary part-time workers who need full-time employment. (Such data produce a three-point-higher unemployment percentage in reports by AFL-CIO and the Urban League.) To get at "hardship," a new national commission

---

1. See John A. Garrity, *Unemployment in History* (New York: Harper & Row, Publishers, 1978), pp. 166–87, 233–36, for a discussion of past and present methods of counting and thereby describing the "unemployed."

headed by Professors Sar A. Levitan and Robert Taggart is proposing an Employment and Earnings Inadequacy Index.

The significance of the current high unemployment figure is much disputed. Many point to the astonishing capacity of the American economy to create new jobs. More than four million jobs were created during 1977 for a total of well over ninety million, surpassing by half Henry Wallace's surprising vision during the 1940s of "sixty million jobs." These critics would prefer to measure the doughnut rather than the hole.[2] Others point to the large influx of women and youth into the labor force, many of whom are not the primary breadwinners in families. Working women now constitute 40% of the labor force; they include half the nation's mothers and five million mothers with children under five. But to lift the lid of these "explanations" is to uncover trends which are in their own way foreboding and are themselves helping to constitute a new state of affairs.

We have scarcely begun to reckon with the fact that 70% of all working women are now single, separated, or heads of households, or are living in families having combined incomes of less than $9,500 per year. Meanwhile, the amount required for the most austere standard of living of a city family of four, according to the United States Chamber of Commerce, has climbed to $10,000. Women's earnings are not "funny money" or "mad money," and in many families the loss of one income can mean the loss of a home.[3]

Similarly, youth employment indicators are very important when we consider that 43% of black youth live in single-parent families. This is to say nothing of the personal and social consequences of present-day "idleness and concupiscence" among the

2. Julius Shiskin, Commissioner of Labor Statistics, compares the merits of measuring employment in "Employment and Unemployment: the Doughnut or the Hole?" *Monthly Labor Review*, February 1976.

3. Cf. Janet L. Norwood, "Some Social Aspects of Unemployment," *News* (Office of Information, U.S. Department of Labor, June 14, 1976). Robert Heilbroner argues that the "middle class" is only half as large in terms of income as it appeared in a Yankelovich survey based on self-perception and residence (the average white working couple just makes it). He predicts a growing struggle in the face of inflation, taxes, and diminished growth. See "Middle-Class Myths and Middle-Class Realities," *Atlantic*, October-November 1976. Rosemary Reuther treats the location of work for working parents in "Working Women and the Male Work Day," *Christianity and Crisis*, February 7, 1977.

young people of society, including the multiplication of single-parent families. One can only speculate concerning the future costs to a society in which three million young people are spending their formative years out of school and out of work.

Proposals for getting people off the welfare rolls and into the job market have not often assessed the increasing pressures of the wage-price structure toward welfare recipiency. Only three out of ten new jobs, according to Eli Ginzberg of the National Manpower Commission, are "good jobs" in the sense that they have a future and can support a family.[4] Many "working poor" labor all year for an income scarcely above the poverty line and fight a losing battle year by year against inflation, felt most severely in the basics of food, shelter, transportation, and health care. Many families feel pressed toward welfare status if only to secure public medical care for themselves and their children. Many youth prefer a combination of welfare checks and street hustle to low-paying dead-end jobs. Thus the objection to counting able-bodied welfare recipients within the labor force raises an ominous question: Are there more and more people for whom, given present trends, there is less and less to do? Are these people who *don't* count? Are we not required to face, in addition to the "cyclical" and "frictional" unemployment held to be characteristic of a free economy, a growing and hardening "structural unemployment" which undermines a free society? The strange word "underclass" now appears without apology on the cover of popular American journals.

The controversy over present unemployment statistics, if pursued, raises questions not only about the *number* of jobs in the economy but about the kind of work needed to afford security to families and communities in the society. In *The Human Condition*, Hannah Arendt pointed to the fact that every Indo-European language, ancient and modern, includes two etymologically unrelated words which sustain a distinction

---

4. Eli Ginzberg, "The Job Problem," *Scientific American*, November 1977. Ginzberg points out that the number of job seekers increases as good jobs open up— as may be seen in the lineups outside employment offices of major firms whenever a notice or rumor of jobs goes out. Sar Levitan argues, and a Rand Corporation Study reports, that nonmoney transfers (food stamps, health services) lift some welfare families above the poverty line.

between "labor" and "work," though modern industrial societies (both Capitalist and Communist) tend to combine their meanings. She distinguished between "the labor of the body," which serves simply to put bread in the laborer's mouth through repetitive motions, and "the work of the hands," by which the worker puts something into his world through inventive activity which secures and qualifies his own existence.[5]

The very strangeness of such a discussion may serve to enforce its point. If we are to pose the new problems enfolded in the present unemployment, perhaps nothing less will do than a fresh exploration of the nature and ends of "work" in human life and of the distinctions between economic, political, and religious activities. We distinguish, as the medievals used to say, in order to unite. Perhaps only on those terms will we be able to take hold of such presently floating questions as "job satisfaction," "vocational education," "the fall of public man," "the problems of leisure," or the present validity of "the Protestant work ethic."

## THE MEANING OF WORK:
## A HISTORICAL REVIEW

The question of work has been historically discussed within every creative society; and reigning notions, practices, and structures of work have been engaged by Hebrews and Christians within many previous cultures. For instance, the classical Greek, Hellenist, and Roman ideal of leisure relegated physical labor to slaves, except for the more refined arts of warfare and agriculture. This view was opposed by Alexandrian Jews as well as by St. Paul, the apostolic fathers, apologists, and monastics East and West.[6] Their opposition was only partly due to the

5. Hannah Arendt, *The Human Condition* (Chicago: University of Chicago Press, 1958), pp. 28–49, 79–96.

6. This opposition is documented in Arthur T. Geoghegan, *The Attitudes Towards Labor in Early Christianity and Ancient Culture* (Washington, D.C.: Catholic University of America Press, 1945); see pp. 229–30. Robert M. Grant, *Early Christianity and Society* (San Francisco: Harper & Row, Publishers, 1977), p. 79, agrees but cites some Stoics who took a similar stand. It should be noted that this countercultural Christian teaching included a listing of jobs which seemed incompatible with faith.

working-class constituency of the synagogues and churches and in fear that nonworkers could become a burden on the community. Their arguments regularly included the biblical commands which combined working with eating (Gen. 3:19; Prov. 6:6–11; 2 Thess. 3:10), solemn admonitions to the soul to avoid idleness and concupiscence, and social obligations to assist the needy and the newcomer—preferably with employment, land, tools, or investment loans which put them in the way of a trade. In opposition to the workless theology and languorous garden of Greek and Roman poets such as Hesiod and Lucretius, they cited the "work" of God and the ordinance of work before as well as after the Fall (Gen. 2:1–3, 15; John 5:17).

The issue of work continued to be dealt with as the early church grew in numbers and maturity. The duty to work became formally related to free activity and contemplation in St. Augustine's *De opere monachorum*, which was concerned with the idleness of certain Carthaginian monks, and became a matter of organization in the widely influential Rule of St. Benedict (Rule XLVIII). While attention to this rule occasionally lapsed, especially with the influx of clergy into the order, reforms of the order invariably revived it. The arguments adduced in behalf of physical labor were basic and universal enough to cause many wealthy persons to forsake their comforts for the tonsure or at least to join the monks in the fields. A new "brotherhood" in labor became firmly enough established to allow former slaves to become popes (Pius I, 140–55, and Callistus I, ca. 223) and to allow a bishop to sell himself into slavery to purchase the freedom of a widow's son (St. Paulinus of Nola, ca. 425). The command in the *Didache* that all should do manual work was so widely and confidently assumed as to require St. Thomas, in an age before movable type, to defend certain monks against the charge that they were wasting all their working time copying books.

The Protestant Reformers of the sixteenth century shared in the widespread reaction of the Renaissance to religious hierarchy and dialectic, though they also criticized the new secularism and cultural optimism. Their polemics against monkish works and contemplation brought them to speak glowingly of ordinary "callings." It should be noted as a qualification, however, that the Reformers meant something broader by "callings" than is ordinarily meant today by "jobs" (they included parenthood, for example) and also something different from what the New Testament usually means by the "calling" of the gospel or of baptism.

Certain cultural historians find in the Reformation a hinge to the modern world of work.[7] But it was subsequent centuries that brought the momentous mechanization and division of labor and the successive displacement of laborers which characterize modern industry. While there has always been poverty, as well as workless and work-shy people, "unemployment" became a term of public discussion only in the 1890s, when systemic fluctuations and decisions displaced great numbers of workers quite apart from natural disaster or personal indolence.[8] The celebrated encyclical *Rerum novarum* of Leo XIII in 1891 was both timely and responsive in its assertion of "a *right* to procure what is required in order to live," along with the traditional duty. If a duty, then a right. This "right" was reasserted by Pius XI in *Quadragesimo Anno*, by Pius XII in 1941, by Pope John XXIII in *Pacem in Terris*, and by the "Pastoral Constitution on the Church in the Modern World" of Vatican II. Similar assertions were made by Protestants who supported the early labor movement and have been repeated by denominations and councils of churches in statements on behalf of full employment during the present decade. On the political scene, this "right" came to expression in the "Four Freedoms" and "Second Bill of Rights" of Franklin Roosevelt, the Employment Act of 1946, the United Nations Universal Declaration of Human Rights of 1948 and the

---

7. Adriano Tilgher, Sebastian de Grazia, R.H. Tawney, Max Weber, and Ernst Troeltsch are among those who have offered this historical judgment. George Forell has pointed to a dilution of the inherent ambiguity in human work on *both* sides of this cultural divide in "Work and the Christian Calling," *Lutheran Quarterly*, May 1956. Thomas F. Green treats the Reformers' view of "vocation" in terms of "lifework" and "lifetime" in *Work, Leisure, and the American Schools* (New York: Random House, 1968), pp. 76–98.

8. On the emergence of this term, see Garrity, *op. cit.*, pp. 4–5, 121–22, 141–42. Corresponding changes in attitude toward worklessness are described pp. 251ff. The first encyclopedic inclusion of "unemployment" occurs in the famous eleventh edition of *Encyclopaedia Britannica* published in 1911.

subsequent Covenant on Social and Economic Rights of 1966, and has been reasserted in arguments supporting the Humphrey-Hawkins legislation (H.R. 50 and S. 50) during recent years.

Our own postclassical, post-Christian, postindustrial world of work is marked by unprecedented circumstances which we have only begun to consider: departure of firms from older cities and regions and even from the nation; increasing inability to compete in steel and hard goods against relative newcomers on the world market; a stubborn structural unemployment in people who are separated both in distance and skills from the machines of society; expansion of services and social welfare programs; high unemployment accompanied by high inflation; costly energy; ominous fiscal strains on a third of the nation's families and on most of the nation's cities.

## PRESENT UNEMPLOYMENT AND
## SOCIAL CHANGE

The past generation has witnessed a rapid transformation, displacement, and movement of work in agriculture and manufacturing. During the twenty-five years before 1968, a full two-thirds of the nation's farm families yielded to the machinery, chemicals, and capital of an expanding agribusiness. Early migration to the cities was infused by a desire to secure a job and, in time, to acquire ownership in a shop. Those small shops themselves have become displaced through development of costly tools and corporate mergers—a development supported by the effectiveness of capital, formerly cheap fuels, and large government programs. Expanding industries did not merely retool and merge; they also moved away. Factory jobs have fled outward from older industrialized cities at a rate more than twice that of the resident blue-collar workers.[9]

Thus we have witnessed a movement of jobs from country to city, from city to suburb, from northern metropolis to sun belt, and from domestic to foreign shops—with workers running to

9. Based on a *Journey to Work* report by the Bureau of the Census in January 1974, which is discussed by Pierre De Vise, "The Suburbanization of Jobs and Minority Unemployment," *Economic Geography*, October 1976.

catch up. Among the casualties are many worker families which find themselves financially unable or reluctant to move. It is one thing to commute downtown by train to an $18,000-a-year desk job; it is quite another thing to commute to the suburbs by automobile to an $8,000-a-year factory job. The movement of industry has cost urban areas large amounts of needed tax revenues, and lost from city neighborhoods are those important second jobs which make use of familiar skills and which make worker families solvent. We should not leave this review of the successive displacement of work in the modern period without observing that the casualties at every stage have been predominantly black or nonwhite.

In addition to all of the above, something very like a loss of work is caused by rising prices. Conventional wisdom during recent decades has correlated inflationary prices with high employment, often citing "the Phillips curve" after a study which compared employment figures with wage rates in England from 1851 to 1967. During this period, unemployment rates were actually reduced through public measures which embraced a higher rate of inflation. But today we find a concurrence of high unemployment with high inflation. We find public measures serving both to keep people out of the work force (as nineteenth-century classical economists warned) and to stimulate the economy (as twentieth-century liberal economists advised). We find strange concurrences of rising prices with diminishing demands, notably in steel and automobile. This has led analysts to trace rising prices not simply to agitation by the work force for higher wages but to high government expenditures and expansion of the money supply, to international wheat deals and ever-expensive oil imports, to the ability of corporations to target profits even when markets decline ("cost-push" as well as "demand-pull"). To this must be added the mushrooming costs of services that enter into the price of everything else.[10]

10. David Warsh et al., "Inflation Is Now Too Serious to Leave to the Economists," *Forbes*, November 15, 1976, and September 15, 1977, speaks of "conflation"—what happens to old costs when new services are added. A General Motors executive complains that the cost of workers' medical benefits now exceeds that of the steel used in the production of its cars.

Such new developments serve to expose certain unforeseen diseconomies in land use for metropolitan expansion. Nearly 15% of the nation's prime agricultural land lies within metropolitan areas. For every such acre paved over, two new acres of marginal land must be brought into farming somewhere else, requiring increased use of petroleum in fertilizers, insecticides, processing, packaging, and delivery.[11] More than half the cost of an ordinary basket of groceries is now traceable to costs of energy. In addition, the change in land use alters the effects of water runoff on water tables and to the costs of water and waste management.

A question arises whether other industrial development has not become obsolescent through new diseconomies of scale and energy use. The notion that every introduction of a laborsaving tool effects an overall economy is subject to reexamination on the basis of public costs involved (investment incentives and bailouts), on the basis of social costs which appear only as side effects and not in the ledgers, and perhaps even on the basis of a comparison between the resources which go into a product and its ultimate uses. Such considerations might lead us to look toward development of enterprises using leaner mixtures of finance, energy, and raw materials, and a richer mixture of labor.[12] They might also lead to consideration of public policies which help trigger that sort of development in disinvested areas.

A new fiscal scarcity characterizes the nation's cities.[13] The scenario is now familiar: removal of industry, rising service costs, municipal borrowing against uncertain future revenues, further disinvestment and flight, and the loss of much that "city" has meant to civilized men and women in the past. Present military and social budgets, accompanied by stubborn inflation and a tax revolt, make any federal "Marshall Plan for the cities" appear extremely unlikely. It seems clear that the new unemployment

11. David Pimental et al., "Land Degradation: Effects on Food and Energy Resources," *Science*, October 8, 1976.
12. For an argument full of advocacy, see Richard Grossman and Gail Daneker, "Jobs and Energy" (Washington, D.C.: Environmentalists for Full Employment, 1977).
13. Donald H. Haider, "Fiscal Scarcity: A New Urban Perspective," in *The New Urban Politics*, ed. Louis N. Masotti and Robert L. Lineberry (Cambridge, Mass.: Ballinger Publishing Co., 1976).

will not be resolved through programs which distribute funds off the top of a growing economy.

The question of the city is once again the classical question of "justice." For justice refers to an appropriate use of scarce resources and to the perpetual interaction of economic, political, and cultural activities.

## THE RECOVERY OF WORK

What are the criteria for policies and actions bearing on the present structural unemployment and the future of work? Paths familiar since World War II are no longer adequate.

It is unlikely that industries will return in sufficient scale to disinvested city areas, though measures to encourage their return or to regulate their flight demand consideration. Nor are we likely to get the metropolitan public transit systems which have been long promised to ameliorate their removal. Ranks of the present unemployed will probably not be reduced substantially simply through investment credits for expansion of present productivity. Such funds often go into machinery rather than people. Subsidies for new workers represent a more direct approach to the unemployed, though the response of industry to such measures has been modest. Heating up the engines of industry beyond a steady rate of growth produces bottlenecks along the line, resulting in diseconomies and higher prices. This is to say nothing of limits which may be imposed at the end of the line by material shortages, foreign competition, or even by saturated markets.

Expansion of services has been the primary means of extending employment and spreading income during the past generation. The hardworking American has become a softworking American almost two to one. Extension of this trend toward "people-work" through public-service jobs, which might protect themselves from public whims through unionization, has suggested itself as the way of providing "meaningful" employment in the future.[14]

14. Brigitte Berger argued for this development in " 'People-Work'—The Youth Culture and the Labor Movement," *Public Interest*, Spring 1974. Policies which foster sponsorship of services by "mediating structures" (neighborhoods, voluntary

It should be noted, however, that the seekers of such "meaningful work" in the past (certainly the finders) have tended to be college graduates. New jobs in major service industries which have been open to newcomers are now sharply curtailed. Vocational counselors caution against matriculation in the education field. Avowed public determination to keep costs of health care to an annual 9% growth would appear to limit job opportunities in that largest service field.

More fundamental considerations will be needed to guide development in the future. Following are some criteria for prospective public policies and measures:

1. These should actually reach unemployed workers and communities most in need. Measures should be "targeted," not rely on "trickle-down."
2. They should contribute to reinvestment and development of self-regenerating enterprises in areas of high unemployment. They should not depend on perpetual public funding.
3. They should require a relatively low use of nonrenewable energy and result in minimal waste. Enterprises may focus increasingly not only on "production" and "consumption" but also on "recovery."
4. They should have more than one sort of output, affording a basis not only for consumption but for chosen activities.
5. They should be conducive to development of families and social institutions, which will then be capable of independent problem posing and problem resolution.

---

associations, churches, parent groups) are advocated by Peter L. Berger and Richard John Neuhaus in *To Empower People* (Washington, D.C.: American Enterprise Institute for Public Policy Research, 1977). If their proposals can be understood as calling for a more equitable *division* of service jobs on the basis of a right to serve as well as to be served, they may indeed point a way forward. But reliance on continued rapid expansion of services in the face of present fiscal realities seems illusory at best. The trenchant argument of Ivan Illich against public expenditures for expansion of services on economic, political, and cultural grounds is summarized in *Toward a History of Needs* (New York: Pantheon, 1978). Similar titles and arguments are to be found in John L. McKnight, "Professional Services and Disabling Help" and "Good Works and Good Work" (Evanston, Illinois: Center for Urban Affairs, Northwestern University, 1977). McKnight speaks of the propensity of services to create need and dependency, to "turn citizens into clients."

A three-mile walk outward from the center of any major city will reveal two decisive propositions that cannot be learned simply by poring over labor statistics or census tracts: (1) the work that most needs doing today is in the very places where people live who most need work; and (2) that work bears on the very basics of life—food, shelter, water, waste, energy. A city with a building stock worth $30 billion, where income and loans have been insufficient to provide maintenance for twenty years, may well require $6 billion worth of work in rehabilitation alone. The challenge becomes one of determining the policies, legislation, organization, and action at various levels which might lead to recovery of such "good work" and to recovery of a market.

If public policies have actually fostered disinvestment of city areas through tax credits and placement of infrastructures in outlying areas (communications, banking, transportation, etc.), might they not also serve to trigger reinvestment in areas where infrastructures are already in place? For this we must avoid reliance on the "quick fix" of emergency job programs or on the "big fix" of capital-absorbing public works. Our five criteria are applicable to citizen activities at many levels: to legislation and regulations which foster redevelopment (investment funds for local development corporations, community land trusts, rehabilitation, food production, research and development conducive to energy conservation), as well as to a review of public works and other public expenditures in terms of job impact and neighborhood impact. Basic to all this is the creation of communities having a social and civic capacity to take advantage of a variety of public measures in ongoing programs of community development—from a use of programs under the Comprehensive Employment and Training Act to development of a new tool kit for neighborhoods and cities.[15]

Professor John Garrity concludes his review of *Unemployment in History* by pointing to a new state of affairs which will require social invention no less than new economic measures: "Clearly,

15. New tools would be characterized by a "multility" rather than "uni-tility" (criterion 4), to use a distinction of Stanley J. Hallett, who describes a central neighborhood multility in "Banking and the Recovery of Prudence," *Church and Society*, April 1977.

the problem calls for social restructuring as well as (probably much more than) economic change. How that can be brought about no one can say with confidence, but efforts to bring it about are more likely to reduce structural unemployment than more direct approaches."[16]

Such social invention is part of the Christian calling. The church repeats a basic conviction that we do not live by bread alone. It begins with the poor. It practices community creation. It knows a rest which gives a point and puts an end to labor. What sharper judgment and action will come to pass when the present problems of unemployment and the future of work are taken up in its walk and conversation?

# Recent Literature

## George H. Brand*

THE POLITICAL ECONOMY OF THE NEW LEFT: AN OUTSIDER'S VIEW
*by Assar Lindbeck. New York: Harper and Row, Publishers, 1977; 102 pp.; $5.95.*

Depending on the ideological perspective of the author, most books that deal with the economics of the New Left tend either to accept uncritically or reject dogmatically the basic tenets of the New Left economists. The book under review is a notable exception. Lindbeck offers a balanced and objective discussion and evaluation of the main economic principles of the New Left.

In the opening chapters Lindbeck examines the New Left critique of academic economists and the way economics is taught

16. Garrity, op. cit., p. 260.
*The author is a Research Associate on the staff of the Department for Church and Society of the Division for Mission in North America, Lutheran Church in America.

at the universities. A major New Left concern is that conventional economists neglect the essential economic problems that confront our society. Among these are, first, the distribution of income, wealth, and economic power. Second, not enough attention is paid to the allocation of resources and the formation of preferences. Third, conventional economists place too much emphasis on the output of commodities and neglect the prior question of the quality of life. In addition, Lindbeck offers a perceptive analysis of the New Left argument that traditional economists have neglected problems of the interaction between economic and political factors.

The author questions the correlation between the structure of ownership and political and social conditions. He recognizes the need, however, for careful studies of the mechanisms which enable pressure groups to obtain privileges through economic and other types of legislation.

ECONOMISTS AT BAY: WHY THE EXPERTS WILL NEVER SOLVE YOUR PROBLEMS
*by Robert Lekachman. New York: McGraw Hill Book Co., 1976; 331 pp.; $3.95.*

From the opening sentence, "As a group economists are slightly more entertaining than bankers and a trifle duller than lawyers," Lekachman offers one of the most incisive analyses of the current state of the economy that one can hope to find. In a prose that is witty, irreverent, and consistently brilliant, he challenges the sacred truisms of the conventional economists. Poverty, inflation, and unemployment are not inherent economic laws of nature. They result from particular social arrangements and the political decisions that perpetuate those arrangements.

Lekachman ridicules the attempt to treat economics as a branch of applied mathematics. The social and economic problems confronting American society will not be resolved by neat mathematical equations. As long as we define full employment in terms of the percent unemployed we have not come to grips with the basic issue. As long as we fail to recognize that corporate pricing practices are a departure from free competition, we will not get a proper handle on the problem of inflation.

What is to be done? Lekachman calls upon economists to relinquish their roles as "neutral" technicians and act like social scientists concerned with human problems. There is no separation between economics and politics. The decisions of political economy must be based on a moral vision.

## PLANNING FOR FULL EMPLOYMENT

*edited by Stanley Moses. Annals of the American Academy of Political and Social Science, no. 418, Philadelphia, 1975; 244 pp.; $4.00.*

Recognizing that unemployment is a personal catastrophe, this issue of the Annals is devoted to a comprehensive discussion of the social, fiscal, and political measures that must be taken in order to create jobs for all those able and willing to work.

The essays are divided into three categories: perspectives on planning and freedom, conceptual and technical issues, and strategic policy problems. The underlying theme is a critique of the economic policy which accepts an inflation-unemployment tradeoff as a means to price stability.

## THE NO-GROWTH SOCIETY

*Daedalus: Journal of the American Academy of Arts and Sciences, Fall 1973; 253 pp.*

Is it possible to determine a proper balance between environmental responsibility and technology-intensive growth? Are there social as well as physical limits to economic growth? This important volume of Daedalus deals with the social, political, and economic implications of zero economic growth. Fourteen essays written by scientists, economists, and humanists debate the changing role of technology in contemporary society and examine how change in size necessitates change in structure. One of the dangers in the growth versus no-growth debate is the tendency to ideologize contrary positions. The issues raised in this volume will be with us for years to come.

THE GRAYING OF WORKING AMERICA: THE COMING
CRISIS OF RETIREMENT-AGE POLICY
*by Harold L. Sheppard and Sara E. Rix. New York: Free Press,
1977; 174 pp.; $12.95.*

This timely book examines an essential dimension of the work
process. A substantive transformation is taking place in America's
population. The authors of this volume project that by the year
2010 there will be a significantly larger proportion of older
nonworkers than today. Conservative estimates suggest that in
the first decade of the twenty-first century there will be over
nineteen million Americans between the ages of sixty-five and
seventy-four.

Given the advances in biomedicine, this group of older
Americans will be able to continue in the productive labor force.
If work is not available, will the younger workers and the private
and public institutions associated with the aged be willing or able
to pay the costs of supporting not only the nineteen million
persons between sixty-five and seventy-four but also the projected
fourteen million Americans seventy-five and older?

Arguing that early retirement is more costly for everyone, the
authors urge that jobs be redesigned to cope with those changing
capacities that are a true consequence of aging. In addition they
call for flexible work schedules as well as continued job information and training programs open to persons of all ages.

This tightly reasoned book deserves the widest possible
audience.


TEN THOUSAND WORKING DAYS
*by Robert Schrank. Cambridge, Mass.: MIT Press, 1978; 243 pp.;
$12.50.*

After forty years in the labor force, the author earned a doctor's
degree in the sociology of work. Schrank's analysis is therefore a
rare combination of the critical techniques of the academician
and the hard-core experiences of a man who has been a factory
worker, a plumber's helper, a farm laborer, a machinist, and an
auto mechanic.

His penetrating analysis suggests that managers tend to be so preoccupied and obsessed with production that they lose concern for workers as people. At times the workers are even viewed as "obstacles" to reaching the managers' objectives. Schrank sees this fact, rather than boredom with the assembly line, as a basic cause of worker alienation.

## THE WORKER AND THE JOB: COPING WITH CHANGE
*edited by Jerome M. Rosow. New York: Columbia University Press, American Assembly Books, 1974; 208 pp.; $2.95.*

Leading experts examine the conflicts between a society that is undergoing rapid and profound change, and the place of work, which remains relatively constant. Various authors explore the changing expectations of today's workers and how dissatisfaction on the job can lead to rising absenteeism and low output. Higher productivity and a better quality of life require that the place, the organization, and the nature of work be improved. Government, unions, and employers are seen as having a shared responsibility in humanizing the work process.

# Work in the Providence of God

## *Foster R. McCurley and John H. Reumann* *

FOR the host of modern problems outlined in Dr. Luecke's challenging article, the Bible may seem to offer little of counsel or even comfort. As with many other social issues, Scripture provides us with no simple prescriptions for twentieth-century enigmas. We cannot expect ancient documents—even those expressions of God's word and will to specific situations—to solve our contemporary dilemma of simultaneous inflation and unemployment. The sociological, political, and economic realities of our day are vastly different from those conditions of the biblical period—diverse as those were, over an almost two-thousand-year span.

Is there more to the contribution of the Bible than to champion "the poor"? (The biblical terms for "poor" can indicate both economic/political and spiritual/religious conditions; eventually they come to mean "the faithful" in Israel.)[1]

*The authors serve as Professors of the Old and New Testaments at the Lutheran Theological Seminary in Philadelphia.

1. C. Umhau Wolf, "Poor," *Interpreter's Dictionary of the Bible* (New York: Abingdon Press, 1962), vol. 3, pp. 843–44; and A. George and other Franciscan biblical scholars, *Gospel Poverty: Essays in Biblical Theology* (Chicago: Franciscan Herald Press, 1977). Some writers "spiritualize" the term *poor* in the New Testament too much. The Franciscan essays warn against several "dead ends" in modern discussions, for poverty "is never a Christian virtue"; there is "no gospel idea of poverty"; but economic deprivation is "an insult to the justice of God" (p. xi).

It must be admitted that biblical theologians have not devoted an over-amount of attention to work and related topics. Alan Richardson produced *The Biblical Doctrine of Work* (1952), a version of which is found in his *Theological Word Book of the Bible* (1950). Swedish scholars like Engnell and Gärtner have especially busied themselves with the theme. Most recently Göran Agrell has sought to distinguish "work," "toil," and "sustenance." But few books on ethics in Old Testament or New touch on our theme, and word studies usually get into questions like "good works and faith" rather than employment and labor. As we shall see, the subject cannot be tackled without attention to the social-economic settings in the biblical world.

Interestingly enough, biblical scholars who have turned to the topic have often done so aware of vigorous discussions going on in society today, particularly in the Christian-Marxist dialogue. Agrell specifically refers (pp. 1–2) to discussion in Sweden on the meaning of being human and of work and to the Marxist view of "man as producer" and of work "as that which makes man human." Richardson (*Word Book*, p. 287) had Marx in mind when he wrote, "The tragedy of our age is that the working classes of the world should have turned their eyes away from the workman of Nazareth and opened their minds to the false gospel of the bourgeois 'scribbler in the British Museum.'"

Modern problems not out of mind, we need in returning to the Bible and its thought to be careful not to claim too much. The contrast between Greco-Roman and Jewish-Christian attitudes toward physical labor affirmed by Geoghegan has already been noted in Dr. Luecke's essay. Geoghegan himself concluded there was "a complete change in the opinion of physical work" in early Christianity. He put it sharply: "For the Greeks, labor was a subhuman, servile activity. . . . The Greek view was adopted by the Romans." Moreover, "the Jewish attitude toward work was nationalistic," limited to Jews (pp. 229–30). Christianity, Geoghegan found, transformed this attitude by stressing the individual and his/her personal perfection (which includes some form of work), charity for others, and eventually work for the unemployed. But Robert M. Grant (p. 79) rightly warns against the exaggeration here, and Geoghegan's own evidence and conclusions show the Greco-Roman view was more varied. (We shall also find the biblical evidence to be more varied too.)

Thus for example in the world of Homer, gods and goddesses labored, much like mortals. The poet Hesiod exhorts, "Work with work upon work." (This was a reflection of necessity in the "iron age," compared to the "golden age" when work was not necessary.) Hercules was famed for his twelve labors. The Roman republic was built upon the sturdy working farmer, and middle-class "know-how" was a hallmark of the empire. The guild movement created a certain satisfaction with good workmanship. Cynics urged emulating Hercules. Dio Chrysostom, the orator, worked at even menial tasks. Stoics preached the need to carry out one's role in the divine economy of the universe.

"Unemployment" may have become a topic for systematic treatment only in the late nineteenth century, but it was a frequent plight in the ancient world. "No one has hired us" was a lament in agricultural Palestine (Matt. 20:7); the urban masses likewise knew what it meant to be without work. We may note the curious fact that Romans like Tacitus blamed Jews for en-couraging idleness: they rest every seventh day, and farmers, he assumed, every seventh year (*Hist.* 5.4)!

Out of this welter of facts, trends, countertrends, and theories, how shall we assess "work" in biblical thought? Four propositions for consideration may guide our examination of the Old and the New Testaments.

1. Work is positively assessed, not just as a curse but as a part of God's intent, yet the Bible does not command it as an absolute. It is not biblical theology to say "Man works to live and lives to work," true as that has seemed in many civilizations and cultures.

2. The Bible also views work negatively, as toil, and sets limits to its sway over humankind. Important as it is to work well—God works, Jesus can be so depicted, Paul continued to practice his trade just as a rabbi would—existence is not just defined by work. And at times we can even feel an "antiwork polemic" running through the biblical witness.

3. There is some merit in distinguishing terms as Agrell seeks to do. *Work* connotes human activity for sustenance. *Toil* has less positive connotations of effort, strain, backbreaking work.

*Sustenance* refers to resources for life, the maintenance of human existence (p. 154, note 18). He also suggests there can be "sustenance without toil" (as in paradise) and "toil without sustenance" (as in a time of catastrophe).

4. In all this there will emerge a dialectical view in the Bible about work, and we have not done justice to the subject unless we have viewed it within the whole of creation *and* from the standpoint of salvation *and* eschatology. But how shall we begin? Not individualistically, but from the standpoint of the people of God.

As a theological book, that is, as a collection of books about God and his relationships with people, the Bible does offer us a context for living out our existence as the people of God. This existence is never portrayed as an escape to Nirvana but is always related to concrete realities of daily life. Whether one examines the Ten Commandments of the Sinai tradition or the ethical imperatives of Romans, the existence wrought by the activity of God involves his people in the arenas of social, political, economic, and legal realities. Moreover, what is stressed are the personal relationships in these realities—relationships to God, to family, to neighbor, to stranger.

The context for the people of God in terms of the specific issues of work and economy is thus the relationship between God and humans. In this relationship work or labor is an activity for both God and the creatures he has made. In the Old Testament there are four Hebrew words used commonly for "work." While one term is used for human activity, because of its connotations of service, slavery, worship, three are employed in verbal and nominal forms to speak of God's activity as well as of human labor and deeds. Our task is to examine the nature of work in its divine and human components.

## WORK AS A PART OF GOD'S CREATION

In the priestly account of creation (Gen. 1:1—2:4a) the work accomplished is exclusively that of God. God brought the heavens and the earth into being, and structured the various phenomena of both realms in such a way that order was established for the continuation of nature and creatures. God's activity throughout the account is speaking; he brings all things into his ordered world by divine fiat. At the same time, however, interspersed throughout the story are the words "make" (1:7, 16, 25, 26, 31; 2:2, 3) and "create" (1:1, 21, 27; 2:3). Thus we should not get the impression that because God spoke creation into being, he did not labor. On the contrary, all that "making" and "creating" was so strenuous that after six days of it, God rested.

The earlier Yahwistic creation story (Gen. 2:4b–25) likewise describes the work of the Lord God as physical labor. The words used are "make" (2:4), "form" as a potter (2:7, 8, 19), "build" (2:22), and "plant" (2:8). In this story, however, work is not exclusively God's. After planting the garden and making it fruitful (an oasis), God "took the man and put him in the Garden of Eden to till it and keep it," literally, to work it and preserve it (2:15).

At first glance the Yahwist seems merely to have taken over from the ancient Near East the concept that humans were created as slaves of the gods. In the famous creation epic from Babylon, the *Enuma elish*, the human race is created and "charged with the service of the gods that they (the gods) might be at ease"! Thus it might seem in Genesis 2 that man's purpose in the garden "to work it and preserve it" follows the same pattern.

In fact the biblical story actually contradicts the notion of humans as slaves and of work as the gods' chores. Note the order of the created things: the man, then the garden. The man was not made to work the garden of God, as in other creation stories. Rather the garden was made by God as a habitable place for the man. Thus the garden is man's, and his work in tilling and preserving the garden is intended for his own benefit. Work is viewed here as part of God's creation and is to be undertaken in the *shalom*-like relationship between God and his human creatures. This work—provided as one of God's blessings, along with food to eat, beauty to behold, and companionship to enjoy—is for human welfare in the world which God worked so hard to create.

Because this work results in human benefit, one is obliged to do it in order to reap its gains. The wisdom literature of the Book of Proverbs stresses repeatedly this necessary correlation; a son who gathers in summer is prudent (10:5); the one who tills the land will have food in abundance (12:11); he who tends a fig tree will eat its fruit (27:18). And quite realistically, it is one's own appetite that urges him on to perform his work (16:26). In characteristic fashion, this wisdom book concludes with the note that fear of the Lord is the basis for heeding the obligations to work and for benefiting from such labor (30:30–31).

Finally, so that human work find its proper place in the order of things (the goal of wisdom teaching), it is necessary that work and plans be committed to the Lord in order to be established (Prov. 16:3). Apart from such a context for human plans and striving, a person might not understand his or her own limitations as well as the providence of God (16:1, 9; 19:21; 20:24). Aware of God's creative nurturing for the world and the creatures he put in it, the human response of doing work to God's glory sets life in the context of the divine-human relationship established by God himself.

Yet this work is not an end in itself. Since its purpose is human welfare and sustenance, work has limits. Just as God rested on the Sabbath day from his creative work, so God commanded rest for his people as they journeyed through the wilderness. In fact, in the priestly narrative of the manna incident in Exodus 16, God assured that the people would not work on the Sabbath; he provided no manna on the seventh day but gave twice as much on the sixth day. Thus not even for the sustenance was God's care for rest diminished. The Decalogue of Exodus 20 likewise includes the apodictic command to rest on the Sabbath day on the basis of God's creation rest. Thus, as important as work is in the Old Testament witnesses, it is not all-encompassing, not a compulsion, not a goal; rather it is a necessary means to other ends such as sustenance and even rest.

In some of the legal codes this rest command benefits not only oneself but others as well. The Book of the Covenant insists that rest on the seventh day extends to ox, ass, bondmaid's son, and alien (Exod. 23:12). Moreover, sabbath rest should include the seventh year when the ground should lie fallow "that the poor of your people may eat" (Exod. 23:10–11; see also Lev. 25:1–7). Only by resting can others rest too; only by resting can others eat.

In this light, rest becomes a social and moral obligation for those who have both jobs and food!

Thus the creation stories provide us with a basic view of work within God's intended order of things created. Within the *shalom*—that is, complete, whole relationship with God— human work is for human benefit. It is sharing in God's creative action; it is thus good. But human work is limited by God's own rest from his labors for the good of self and of others.

## WORK AS TOIL BECAUSE OF SIN

The condition of harmony lasted only as long as "the afternoon of the first day" (Luther). Then, due to the seductive reasoning of the clever serpent, the woman and the man chose to break down the barrier between Creator and creature and strove to "be like God, knowing good and evil" (Gen. 3:5). Because of the desire to be free of all imposed restraints, the relationship between God and the human pair was changed. No more did *shalom* prevail. Now death, the absence of the complete life with God, took over, and the couple was banished from the garden. Then God spoke his curse on the ground: "in toil you shall eat of it (the ground) all the days of your life" (Gen. 3:17); and again, "In the sweat of your face you shall eat bread" (v. 19). In this broken relationship with God, the work which was so good before now becomes "toil." The same word for "toil" occurs in some cases for physical pain; usually both the verbal and nominal forms refer to such emotional anguish as that of a forsaken wife (Isa. 54:6), a mourning father (2 Sam. 19:3), an exiled people (Isa. 14:3), or a broken spirit (Prov. 15:13). Thus it is not simply that work becomes physically strenuous due to humankind's rebellion against God; presumably work involved muscular stress from the beginning. Now work becomes the proverbial "pain in the neck" outside the harmonious relationship with the Creator.

Sin also is the cause of the fruitlessness or vanity of work. The Book of Deuteronomy is structured along the lines of ancient suzerain-vassal treaties, under terms of which the suzerain (here the Lord) imposes curses or blessings on the vassal (here Israel) depending on whether or not the vassal was obedient to the stipulations set forth. Deuteronomy 12—26 lists the code of laws which the Lord gave to Israel. Then the series of blessings and curses follow in chapters 27—28. Among the curses is the sequence at 28:30–46 which spells out the fruitlessness of work: Israel shall build houses but not dwell in them, plant vineyards but not eat their produce, raise livestock for the enemy's food— the sight of which will drive Israel mad (toil?). In exile— understood as God's judgment on Israel's unfaithfulness—the people will plant seeds, dress vineyards, tend to the olive trees, but locusts, worms, and diseases will prevent any enjoyment of harvest. All this "because you did not obey the voice of the Lord your God, to keep his commandments and his statutes which he commanded you" (Deut. 28:45).

While it speaks of folly rather than sin, the Book of Proverbs emphasizes that laziness or slothfulness will reap only disaster. The son who sleeps instead of working during harvesttime will bring shame upon himself (10:5). An idle person will earn no food and thus suffer hunger (19:15). While industry brings its own rewards, so does idleness reap its appropriate recompense on the "fool."

Yet the proverbs move one step beyond this doctrine of rewards and punishments to deal with the suffering of the poor at the hands of others. It is other people's "foolishness" that causes some to suffer misfortune and injustice. While there are numerous individual proverbs dealing with the necessity of caring for the poor and with the folly of failing to do so, one in particular stands out to speak to our concern about work and its benefits.

> The fallow ground of the poor yields much food,
> but it is swept away through injustice.
>
> (Prov. 13:23)

Thus the difference between the haves and the have-nots is not simply work or idleness but injustice done to those who have so little to begin with. Such an insight prevents any oversimplified judgment on the laziness of the poor, which seems to be possible on the basis of some of the proverbs above and on the basis of some modern-day "wisdom."

Thus because of sin the work God gave to humans becomes toil and anguish; it results in fruitlessness when judgment from God gives Israel's labor to other peoples and when injustice from fellow humans deprives the poor even of food. Such is work in God's creation gone askew!

## WORK IN THE NEW CREATION

It is little wonder that as Israel looked forward to that eschatological moment when God would establish his kingship over all, the prophets spoke of a new creation—one like the first, before the Fall. The last two chapters of the Book of Isaiah— assigned to Third Isaiah—are eloquent in their hymnic-like description of new heavens and a new earth. No more weeping, no more distress; now there will be gladness and joy. But it is still no Nirvana! People will continue to die, but not prematurely! People will continue to work, but not in vain.

> They shall build houses and inhabit them;
>     they shall plant vineyards and eat their fruit.
> They shall not build and another inhabit;
>     they shall not plant and another eat;
> for like the days of a tree shall the days of my people be,
>     and my chosen shall long enjoy the work of their hands."
>                                                 (Isa. 65:21–22)

This powerful expression of the fruitfulness of labor in the new creation reverses the curse announced as judgment on those who disobeyed the law (Deut. 28:30ff.). No longer shall others profit from one's labors; in the kingdom to come—down-to-earth as it is—each person will enjoy the results of his and her labor. To Israel—tossed about from one world empire to another, paying tribute to a series of powerful kingdoms, watching its land occupied by strangers, and working hands to the bone on someone else's turf—such a view of new heavens and a new earth was good news indeed! "My chosen shall long enjoy the work of their hands."

## WORK AND SALVATION

Until now we have examined the role of work in the area of creation and new creation. At this point we move to consider the place of work in the area of salvation—in historical events which free Israel from bondage and bring her into a new relationship with God.

The so-called historical creeds of the Hexateuch summarize the events which led Israel to become the people of God. At Deuteronomy 6:21–23, a father is to teach his son about the exodus from Egypt according to a pattern which describes the people's condition in Egypt as one of slavery, and the deliverance solely in terms of God's work. Again, Deuteronomy 26:5b–9 offers a similar summary to be recited when offering the first-fruits before the altar: the people's condition of slavery is followed by God's work of bringing the people out of Egypt and into the land of Canaan. Joshua 24:2–13, an expanded historical summary, speaks of God in the first person as the one who worked in multiplying the people, plaguing Egypt, bringing Israel across the Red Sea, and giving them the land.

This exclusive work of the Lord is demonstrated further by the Holy War formulas by which God defeated Israel's enemies in bringing Israel out of Egypt and into the land of Canaan. "The Lord will fight for you; you have only to be still" (Exod. 14:14). "Do not fear them, for I have given them into your hands" (Josh. 10:8). Thus the entire deliverance complex of exodus-wilderness-conquest is solely the work of God.

Startlingly, some texts move beyond this description of salvation as God's work alone to list the benefits Israel will reap from other people's work. At the end of the historical summary of Joshua 24:2–13, the Lord's speech through Joshua announces, "I gave you a land on which you had not labored, and cities which you had not built, and you dwell therein; you eat the fruit of vineyards and oliveyards which you did not plant" (v. 13). Here as part of God's gift of the land—which previously belonged to other peoples—benefits come to Israel without her own work.

Indeed if Israel forgets this gift of God, "when you have eaten and are full, and have built goodly houses and live in them, and when your herds and flocks multiply," then Israel is to beware that she thinks her own power and might have acquired this wealth (Deut. 8:12–18). All the goodness of labor is Israel's only because God is faithful to the covenant he made with the fathers. Thus Israel may not boast even of her own work in the land. Such indeed is the Old Testament emphasis on the exclusive work of God in the realm of redemption.

To conclude, "work" in the Old Testament view is ambiguous. On the one hand it is a good and necessary part of God's creation; on the other hand it is toil because of sin. On the one hand work leads to benefits; on the other hand injustice can deprive the poor of the fruits of their work. On the one hand work is vital in continuing the world's order; on the other hand it is limited by rest. On the one hand work is cooperating with God in creation; on the other hand work is exclusively God's in redemption.

Perhaps for us who wait a final consummation of God's kingdom with new heavens and a new earth but who are yet very much in this world, Jeremiah's letter to the exiles in Babylon offers helpful advice. While promising redemption, that is, return from Babylon to Jerusalem, in due course (seventy years), God admonishes the exiles in the meantime: "Build houses and live in them; plant gardens and eat their produce, . . . multiply there, and do not decrease. But seek the welfare of the city where I have sent you into exile, and pray to the Lord on its behalf, for in its welfare you will find your welfare" (Jer. 29:5-7). The covenant curse has befallen the people: God has taken them into exile in a land not theirs. And yet even in their toil the exiles can enjoy the fruits of labor as they live in the world where they are. In Babylon they do their work and they pray—for Babylon's sake and their own. And yet the last word is not their work but God's: he gives them a future and a hope by promising them deliverance and homecoming.

## TOWARD A NEW TESTAMENT PICTURE

This rich and varied Old Testament understanding of work continued to develop in the ensuing centuries of Judaism which led to the New Testament era. In general the Old Testament themes were carried on: work is a way of serving God, it provides sustenance, yet it can be hard and laborious toil. In particular these later centuries when Judaism was emerging stressed that work done in righteousness leads to a blessing but work done in ungodliness is under a curse (Wisd. of Sol. 3:15; Ecclus. 11:18-19; cf. Luke 12:15-21).

The Old Testament's ambivalence about work can be seen in the books of the Apocrypha and Pseudepigrapha. Sirach (Ecclesiasticus) is an illustration. "Stand by your covenant" and "keep at your work" are parallel bits of advice (11:20). "Toilsome labor and farm work" were created by the Most High, for servant and master alike (7:15; cf. 7:20). Work keeps people out of mischief (33:24–28). Yet labor is regarded as laborious, and the point in chapter 17 of the retelling of the Genesis 1—3 story seems to be that more important than dominion over the earth and the work responsibility it implies is occupying oneself with the law of life which God gave (Agrell, p. 34).

As the rabbis sought to apply the law to more and more of life, they too deepened and developed the Old Testament teachings about work. It now became a command, "Love work" (Pirke Aboth 1.10). The Divine Presence was aid to rest on manual labor (Tos. Men. 7.8). Study of the law was also regarded as proper toil under a Taskmaster who rewards labor (Aboth 2.18). Very significant for the New Testament was the rabbinic practice that each rabbi know a trade, to work with his hands. Sometimes there were debates about the relation between daily work and study of Torah, and sometimes a feeling of superiority for the letter. But all in all, rabbinic Judaism looked at work through positive eyes. "Work is a splendid thing" (Gittin 67b).

From this background Jesus and early Christianity are frequently interpreted portraying an affirmative view of work. Jesus was a carpenter (Mark 6:3, "worker, craftsman"—it is immaterial to our picture if the term should mean "stonemason" or "artisan"; the point is, Jesus worked at a trade). His father likewise was a carpenter (Matt. 13:55). His disciples he chose from the working classes—fishermen, tax collectors, and the like—and if they were not poor and of the lowest groups, they were petite bourgeoisie and knew the struggle of hard work. He could appreciate and feel at home with the rich, yet outcastes flocked to him.

Jesus' teachings often reflect the workaday world of Palestine. The parables smack of farms and laborers and crops. He could allude to making yokes as a carpenter might (Matt. 11:29). He knew toil and talked of a creator God who worked and continued to care providentially for his world: "My Father is working still, and I am working" (John 5:17). The latter verse is part of a defense for Jesus' working cures on the Sabbath; it reflects the idea of Psalm 121:4 that even though God too observed Sabbath (Gen. 2:3), he never ceased maintaining the universe; so Jesus too works for human well-being, even on the Sabbath day. Agrell treats as the paradigmatic passage of the Synoptics the discourse on anxiety in Luke 12:22–31 (parallel Matt. 6:25–34) about trust in God's providence even as one works for sustenance.

Paul and the early church continued this attitude. True, in Thessalonica there were those who stopped working because they expected the parousia any moment. But by and large Christians were hardworking and industrious. Paul worked with his hands to support his mission work, like any rabbi. He was a tentmaker (Acts 18:3, or leatherworker; cf. 1 Cor. 9:4–15). He rebuked the Thessalonians with the dictum "No work, no eats" (2 Thess. 3:10). Thus was laid the foundation, in our Lord and the first fathers in the faith, for a solid work ethic. Paul's advice to Timothy about being "a good workman before God who needs not be ashamed" became a model for all Christians in their daily work (2 Tim. 2:15).

## JESUS AND HIS DISCIPLES: ITINERANTS?

More recent scholarship has amplified or questioned segments of this picture from biblical theology. Jesus may have been trained as a carpenter, but the New Testament Gospels never show him working at a trade during his ministry. Jesus instead travels about Galilee proclaiming that the kingdom of God is coming.

Working sociologically, Gerd Theissen has pointed to a number of Synoptic texts where Jesus seems a wandering charismatic. His disciples are assumed to be itinerants too. They are homeless (Mark 1:16; 10:28; Matt. 8:20), without family (Mark 10:29; 1:20), without possessions of their own (Matt. 10:10), and severe in their critique of riches (Luke 6:24–25). Yet they trust in God and his providential care, at the mercy of the world but in God's hands (Matt. 5:38–39, 41; 10:17ff.). While sympathizers like

Mary and Martha or Simon the leper remain at their daily work, opening their homes to Jesus and his disciples, the wandering messengers go about preaching the urgent message of God's coming reign.

Theissen contrasts Jesus and his followers to the rigidly disciplined but economically productive Qumran community and the Zealot resistance fighters with their program of revolutionary change and debt cancellation. The Jesus movement was ambivalent toward possessions and wealth accumulated by work: it criticized riches (Mark 10:25) yet lived off such wealth (Luke 8:3; Mark 15:43). Jesus thus created a reform movement which relaxed some norms (such as those about "work" on the Sabbath) and intensified others (e.g., renunciation of possessions), and above all stressed love. Because of the imminent kingdom the job was to go and preach, even at the cost of one's normal work and social-economic ties.

Enough statements of this sort are preserved in the Q tradition to suggest that Jesus' disciples must have in many cases been like this, and Jesus himself likely gave up the carpentry shop for the itinerant preacher's life. To this extent Jesus and his disciples do not fit the current mold. Theologically they reflect an attitude toward labor characteristic of the new creation or an expectation of God's care such as Israel had experienced while wandering in the wilderness. To this extent the foreshortened eschatological expectancy of early Christianity may have contributed to a critique of worldly labor and human toil.

## THE CONTRIBUTION OF PAUL

Wandering preachers of the sort we have just described must have been a phenomenon for decades in the early church. The Didache both warns against and appreciates itinerants (11:3–6; 12:1–5; 10:7): two or three days of free hospitality for them but no money, and if one settles among you, "Let him work and eat." The preachers who turned up in Paul's Corinth may have been akin to the itinerants of the Q tradition. Christianity thus had an "antiwork" tendency stemming from its eschatological impulse to "go and preach the new things God was doing." Such a theme may have been especially welcome in the Hellenistic world with its inclinations not to work. It is out of this situation that some of Paul's admonitory sections arise, for Paul and Barnabas function more as "community organizers" (Theissen).

In 1 Thessalonians 4:9–12, as part of his ongoing teaching, Paul urges work—not as divine command but because it results in independence from others, resources with which to show love, and respect from outsiders. Paul here sees daily work as a sphere where one has positive contact with the world. It is service to God and others while awaiting the day of the Lord. One buys and sells and deals with the world, but as if that world were not the ultimate, for it is passing away (1 Cor. 7:29–31).

It is at this point that we note Paul's positive contribution from his rabbinic heritage. Although he recognized the right of legitimately authorized preachers to be supported by their congregations, he gave up such a right in order to support himself by his own labor. Acts 19:9 in the Western text addition suggests the romantic detail that Paul may have worked "normal hours" at his trade in Ephesus but used the hall of Tyrannus to teach at the hot time of day, 11 A.M. to 4 P.M., when it was available perhaps more cheaply! In 1 Corinthians 9 we hear Paul arguing his case against the views of other missionaries that for him manual labor is a part of his missionary work. Work physically is still toil and no direct service to God, but it allows him to serve without burdening others and may be an arena of witness (9:19–23). Agrell even thinks the "toil" Paul mentions in his list of eschatological sufferings (2 Cor. 11:23, 27, "labors") includes his manual labor. If so, work has been incorporated into "the life formed by Christ and anticipating the end" (p. 115).

Agrell, in line with much modern scholarship, also arranges other Pauline passages on work in a chronological course of development by assuming some are deutero-Pauline. Second Thessalonians 3:6–15 then faces a situation a little different than that in 1 Thessalonians: some brethren have stopped working because they think the future coming of the Lord Jesus Christ is already at hand. "Not yet," replies chapter 2; in the interim God's will is that church people work to sustain themselves (3:6ff.), not exploiting others, not growing weary of well-doing (3:11–13). Paul's own example is specifically cited (3:7–9). To work is part of apostolic tradition (3:10). Life since the Fall (Gen. 3:17–19, possibly alluded to in 2 Thess. 3:10 and elsewhere) may be "second best," but it is the "natural order" which eschatology has not yet superseded.

Ephesians 4:28 goes a step further: "Let the thief no longer steal, but rather let him labor, doing honest work with his hands, so that he may be able to give to those in need." Paul, in his genuine letters, pleads for work within his missionary purpose. Second Thessalonians, while holding fast to the future hope, sees work as God's will in the natural order. Ephesians, with its emphasis upon the "now" of the church as the time of salvation, speaks even more positively of work (as it does of marriage) and adds it is necessary for producing something to give to others. The Pastorals assume work as part of God-given reality, with no eschatological critique of it: it is a means of serving God by sharing with others (see especially 1 Tim. 6:17).

An interesting final picture comes in the speech of Paul to the Ephesian elders at Acts 20:33–34. Paul gave an example by toiling with his hands so as to "help the weak," thus fulfilling a beatitude from Jesus(!): "To give, as a result of our work, is blessed." We have thereby come to terms with life in the workaday world in a manner different from that of Jesus and his first disciples. Eschatology thus conditions a doctrine of work.

If there is anything to these lines of development from Jesus and his followers to Paul and to the deutero-Paulines and Luke, we have found that New Testament Christianity is affirming *and* critical of work, ambivalent *and* dialectic, just as our Old Testament evidence and initial propositions suggested. Subsequent theology is not bound to a six- or five-day workweek; labor counts but is not the ultimate.

This brings us to the concluding consideration: How should the church present such materials to people today? Of course, the preacher has an opportunity in the secular calendar on Labor Day. But what about the rest of the year? Perhaps the best approach is an educational forum featuring give-and-take among the participants in discussions of such topics as biblical attitudes toward work, modern economics, and challenges in the contemporary labor market.

## REFERENCE BIBLIOGRAPHY

Agrell, Göran. *Work, Toil and Sustenance: An Examination of the View of Work in the New Testament, Taking into Consideration Views Found in Old Testament, Intertestamental, and Early Rabbinic Writings.* Lund: Verbum, Håkan Ohlssons, 1976.

Engnell, Ivan. "Some Biblical Attitudes to Work. 1. Work in the Old Testament." *Svensk Exegetisk Arsbok* 26 (1961), pp. 5–12. See also Gärtner, below.

Gärtner, Bertil. "Work in the New Testament," *Svensk Exegetisk Arsbok* 26 (1961), pp. 13–18. Cf. *New Testament Abstracts* 7:744. The Old Testament attitude is basically negative, and the New Testament elaborates no doctrine as such.

Grant, Robert M. "Work and Occupations," in *Early Christianity and Society: Seven Studies.* New York: Harper & Row, Publishers, 1977, pp. 66–95.

Hengel, Martin. *Property and Riches in the Early Church: Aspects of a Social History of Christianity.* Philadelphia: Fortress Press, 1974. Especially pp. 23–30 on Jesus' radical critique of property and pp. 60–64 on "the compromise of effective compensation" in a positive evaluation of manual labor.

*Interpreter's Dictionary of the Bible.* New York: Abingdon Press, 1962. C. R. North, "Works of God, the," vol. 4, pp. 872–73. C. U. Wolf, "Labor," vol. 3, pp. 51–52.

Richardson, Alan. *The Biblical Doctrine of Work.* London: Student Christian Movement Press, 1952. More briefly, "Work, Labour," in *A Theological Word Book of the Bible.* New York: Macmillan Co., 1950, pp. 285–87.

*Theological Dictionary of the New Testament* (ed. G. Kittel). G. Bertram, "*ergon,* etc.," vol. 2, pp. 635–55. F. Hauck, "*kopos,* etc.," vol. 3, pp. 827–30.

Theissen, Gerd. *Sociology of Early Palestinian Christianity.* Philadelphia: Fortress Press, 1978. Also important is his "Legitimation und Lebensunterhalt: Ein Beitrag zur Sociologie urchristlicher Missionare." *New Testament Studies* 21 (1974–75), pp. 192–221, summarized in *New Testament Abstracts* 19:1154.

# Work as Praise

## William H. Lazareth *

YOU can tell a lot about people by their slogans and wisecracks. The spirit of an age is often reflected in the proverbial wisdom which people accept as "common sense," however uncommon and senseless it may be. Those ideas which are taken for granted give us a rather revealing picture of the "working philosophy" of the typical person on the street.

Since these slogans come and go, no list of them could ever be considered final. Nevertheless, it should open our eyes to recall some of the more popular maxims of recent years. By stretching the point a bit we might call them the "ten commandments" of godless people.

1. Don't be a sucker.
2. Enjoy yourself; it's later than you think.
3. The world owes me a living.
4. So what! Everybody's doing it.
5. Look out for yourself; nobody else will.
6. Everything is relative anyhow.
7. Just don't rock the boat.
8. You can't fight city hall.
9. All's fair in love and war.
10. Well, it works!

All of these sayings are deeply rooted in the modern "great commandment": "It's not what you believe but how you live that really counts." In a century torn to pieces by world wars,

*An earlier version of this revised and expanded essay is included in the author's *Helping Youth and Adults Know Doctrine* (Philadelphia: Lutheran Church Press, 1963), pp. 125ff.

depressions, revolutions, and racial strife, people are impatient
with visions of "pie in the sky by and by." They want deeds, not
creeds. They seek concrete programs, not empty promises.

While this moral indignation should give Christians cause for
real soul-searching, the secular world's proposed remedy remains
an illusion. Even though its ethical record is far from what it
should be, the church must still proclaim that ethical fruits are
determined by religious roots. Whether people are Communists,
Nazis, or Christians, it is their character that shape their conduct
as they put beliefs into action.

In theological language, we are faced here with the problem of
the relation of justification to sanctification. More simply, how
does God's love for us inspire our love for one another?

## ALL CHRISTIANS ARE SAINTS

Christians confess that the church of Jesus Christ is holy. That
is, the church is the "communion of saints" in which men and
women empowered by the Holy Spirit are declared and made
righteous by God's grace.

Strictly speaking, Christianity asserts that the holiness consists
solely in its gracious Head and not in the moral perfection of its
members. God's command, "Be perfect, even as I am perfect"
(Matt. 5:48), convicts all persons of sin. As we trust in a Savior for
pardon and renewal, our life in the Spirit is one of continual
repentance, daily death and rebirth. We have been declared
righteous for Christ's sake alone. This divine pardon constitutes
our *justification*. Because of Calvary, God has graciously forgiven
and accepted us despite our sin.

Once we are accepted, God's Holy Spirit starts to make us as
righteous as he has already declared us to be. This divine renewal
constitutes our *sanctification*. The prisoner who has been freely
acquitted is now just as freely rehabilitated. The same holy God
who justified us by grace through faith now sanctifies us by grace
through love.

Like birth and growth, these two movements are distinguish-
able in logic but inseparable in life. Once liberated from the rule
and guilt of sin, the reborn baptized Christian starts at once to

grow in grace. That is, he/she begins to live out of the resources of God's bounty, confident that "he who began a good work in you will bring it to completion at the day of Jesus Christ" (Phil. 1:6).

Whereas our justification takes place the moment we are graciously accepted by God in Christ, our sanctification remains a lifelong process of renewal. Daily the "old Adam" must be crucified; daily the "new Adam" is resurrected. Sin continues to persist in the hearts of redeemed persons to the end of their days. Christians never reach moral perfection in this life. Nevertheless, the Holy Spirit is constantly active within them, doggedly restoring them to the holy and loving image of God in which they were created.

This means that every Christian is at once both righteous and sinful. This is not a quantitative matter which might conceivably shift in percentage from 60–40 to 80–20, when one agrees to teach a church-school class, for instance. Consequently, the whole Christian life is a continual "crawling back into our baptism" (Luther). Christians are wholly righteous insofar as they trust in Christ, and yet wholly unrighteous insofar as they still worship false gods. Sinful in self and yet righteous in Christ, they are in continual need of the saving word of God both to bolster their faith and to fire their love.

Now we can understand why Paul is able to address all believing Christians (in Galatia, Rome, and Corinth) as "saints." The saints are the "elect of God"—whatever their persisting ethical shortcomings—whom the Holy Spirit has called into consecrated discipleship. In the Bible, saints are described as the "temples of God" in whom the Holy Spirit works pardon for salvation and power for service. We confess the true faith whenever we declare that the "holy catholic (Christian) church" is also the "communion of saints"—in the words of the Apostles' Creed.

## THE CHRISTIAN'S ETHICAL LIFE-STYLE

The basic issue of the Reformation was the sovereignty of this law-free gospel in the church, not confusing that gospel with

God's law. In the New Testament, the gospel is a message of "good news." It announces the "glad tidings" that God has culminated his saving events in history with the life, death, and resurrection of Jesus Christ. It tells of what Christ has done to free us from sin and reconcile us with God. But in late medieval Catholicism, the gospel was interpreted as giving new instructions concerning how we should act according to God's law. The accent shifted from what Christ has done for us to what we must do for him. Christ was viewed as "a new Moses" and the gospel became a "new law."

How did this confusion of law and gospel take place? Rome based its approach on Jesus' pre-Calvary saying, "Think not that I have come to abolish the law and the prophets; I have not come to abolish but to fulfill them" (Matt. 5:17). The gospel was viewed primarily as a clearer form of the sovereign law of God. God's "old testament" with Israel found no radical correction but only gradual fulfillment in his "new testament" in Christ. Totally underestimated was John's post-Calvary witness, "The law was given through Moses; grace and truth came through Jesus Christ" (1:17).

The late medieval church taught that Christ had offered his sufferings and death to God as a sacrifice in satisfaction for humanity's original sin. Along with those of morally exceptional saints, the merits earned by Christ's passion were at the church's disposal. Therefore, primarily through administration of the sacraments, God's grace could now be infused like medicine into persons in order to empower them to contribute to their salvation by the performance of meritorious good works.

On this legalistic basis, Rome established a double standard of Christian piety. Laypersons were expected to obey only the "general commandments" of the Decalogue (no killing, adultery, stealing), whereas "the religious" had to vow to live in accord with the higher "counsels of perfection" of the Sermon on the Mount (poverty, celibacy, and obedience). This was considered to be the perfect fulfillment of the holy law of God.

The net result of this was to corrupt God's plan of salvation. Christianity had been corrupted into an uncertain religious venture in which salvation must be partially earned rather than faithfully accepted as a totally free gift of God's grace.

Following the New Testament, the Reformers taught that the good we do does not in any way influence our justification. "For we hold that a man is justified by faith apart from works of law" (Rom. 3:28). A person, always proud, likes to think he has something to do with his salvation. He does not. It is faith alone that apprehends God's grace and forgiveness. But that same faith will naturally and necessarily result in loving service to one's neighbors. Good works do not justify, but they are the inevitable fruit of being justified. Loveless faith is as unchristian as faithless love. In Luther's words,

> Oh, faith is a living, busy, active, mighty thing, so that it is impossible for it not to be constantly doing what is good. Likewise, faith does not ask if good works are to be done, but before one can ask, faith has already done them and is constantly active. Whoever does not perform such good works is a faithless man. . . . It is therefore as impossible to separate works from faith as it is to separate heat and light from fire.

When we distinguish so sharply between law and gospel, we are not severing ethics from religion and asking persons to choose between them. Instead, we are contrasting two completely different ways of salvation. The legal way is false. The law represents a legal relation to God. It is inward and upward in direction and self-seeking in spirit. Here the theory is that persons help to earn their salvation through works as well as faith. Under the law, persons serve their neighbors grudgingly *in order to* be saved. The gospel, on the other hand, represents an evangelical relation to God. It is downward and outward in direction and self-giving in spirit. Here God offers salvation to us as a free gift of grace and then empowers us to help others just as freely in faithful love. Under the gospel, Christians serve their neighbors willingly *because* they have been saved.

The responsible freedom proclaimed by Paul is normative for Christian ethics. Baptized saints are to live lawfully but not legalistically, freely but not licentiously. "Live as free men, yet without using your freedom as a pretext for evil" (1 Pet. 2:16).

This means that Christian ethics is concerned first and foremost with a new style of life. Christ did not bring his followers an armful of new rules, but came to give life abundantly. We should not concern ourselves initially with what we should do, but rather with what we should be. Again, if the religious roots are good, ethical fruits will follow.

To reduce the Christian faith to a code morality of commandments and, still worse, of prohibitions, is a tragic betrayal of the spirit of Christ. "Love!" was his great commandment, because he knew that ethical demonstration is determined by religious motivation. The Pharisees received his strongest condemnation because their obedient hands were not empowered by loving hearts. The same blade can be plunged into the same body by either a criminal or a surgeon. The motive makes all the difference in the world.

Consequently, the Christian pays far less attention to ethical rules and regulations (though they have their restraining place), than to his growth "to mature manhood, to the measure of the stature of the fullness of Christ" (Eph. 4:13). The Reformers could sum up the difference between these two opposing views of sanctification by contrasting "works of the law" and "fruits of the Spirit" (e.g., *Formula of Concord*, Art. VI).

Insofar as we remain sinful, we are still completely subject to the civil and religious demands of God's law. The law compels us to serve each other, even if only out of fear of punishment or hope of reward. Christians are not perfectionists; they confess their lifelong need of the check of God's law. Since "believers are not fully renewed in this life but the Old Adam clings to them down to the grave, the conflict between Spirit and flesh continues in them."

Insofar as we are righteous, however, Christians are completely free from the curse of the law, to exercise faith actively in love.

> When a person is born anew by the Spirit of God and is liberated from the law (that is, when he is free from this driver and is driven by the Spirit of Christ), he lives according to the immutable will of God as it is comprehended in the law, and, in so far as he is born

anew, he does everything from a free and merry spirit. These works are, strictly speaking, not works of the law but works and fruits of the Spirit, or, as St. Paul calls them, the law of the mind and the law of Christ. According to St. Paul, such people are no longer under law but under grace (Rom. 6:14; 8:2).

*(Formula of Concord,* Art. VI)

Hence, a Christian ethic based upon the grace of God preserves the freedom of believers under the guidance of the Holy Spirit through the Bible, the church, and prayer, to discover anew in each concrete situation what loving "fruits of the Spirit" the will of God permits or requires then and there.

## ALL CHRISTIANS ARE PRIESTS

This evangelical theology of sanctification found practical expression in the doctrine of the church's universal priesthood. In conscious opposition to the clericalism of Rome, the Reformers stressed the calling (vocation) of all baptized Christians to become priests to their neighbors, mediating to them the love of God.

According to Holy Scripture, the term *vocation* is basically religious (rather than economic) and essentially corporate (rather than individual). God calls out a people through a covenant for his redemptive purposes. In the Old Testament this community is Israel; in the New Testament it is the church.

For example, just before Moses was given the Ten Commandments in their personalized "Thou shalt not" form, God established his covenant with all the children of Israel.

Thus you shall say to the house of Jacob, and tell the people of Israel: You have seen what I did to the Egyptians and how I bore you on eagles' wings, and brought you to myself. Now therefore, if you will obey my voice and keep my covenant, you shall be my possession among all peoples; for all the earth is mine, and you shall be to me a kingdom of priests and a holy nation.

(Exod. 19:3–5)

The New Testament both radically corrects and fulfills the Old Testament in its twofold witness to Jesus Christ as the church's true High Priest and to all baptized Christians as constituting his royal priesthood.

The Book of Hebrews, for instance, declares Christ to be "high priest of the good things that have come" (9:11ff.). This is because the sacrificial Lamb of God "entered once for all into the Holy Place, taking not the blood of goats and calves but his own blood, thus securing an eternal redemption." Although he is a divine King, Christ has voluntarily emptied himself of his royal glory and taken on the form of the humble Suffering Servant of God. As the gracious "mediator of a new covenant," Christ acts as the High Priest of the church, the new Israel of God.

With salvation a free gift of divine grace, it follows that Christians do not need to make any kind of propitiatory sacrifices to God. If a priest is a mediator between God and humans, then all Christians are priests because we all serve God by serving each other. God does not need to help, but people do. Consequently, 1 Peter declares that in God's "new Israel," the church, all baptized Christians are incorporated into "a chosen race, a royal priesthood, a holy nation, God's own people" (2:9).

Faithful Christians are empowered by God's indwelling Holy Spirit to love one another as Christ first loved us. He came not to be served but to serve. After Christ humbly washed the feet of the Twelve, he asked, "Do you know what I have done to you? . . . I have given you an example, that you also should do as I have done to you" (John 13:15). Likewise, "By this all men will know that you are my disciples, if you have love for one another" (13:35). As Christ's whole life took the form of a Suffering Servant's, so must ours. In Paul's words, "I appeal to you therefore, . . . by the mercies of God, to present your bodies as a living sacrifice, holy and acceptable to God, which is your spiritual worship" (Rom. 12:1).

It is important to stress again that the Christian ethic of faith active in love is not based on rigid rules but upon a risen Ruler. "For freedom Christ has set us free" (Gal. 5:1) means that Christians do not have merits to earn, rules to obey, principles to apply, or ideals to realize. We have rather a living Lord who calls us to personal discipleship in all areas of life. In God's loving service we find perfect freedom.

64952

We should also note that the Christian ethic is not based upon the naive question, "What would Jesus do in this situation?" To be sure, Christ did leave us a pattern that we should follow in his steps. But this does not mean that we are to try to imitate the deeds of the earthly Jesus. He had his own unique calling as the Messiah to inaugurate the kingdom of God. What we are to do is to imitate the obedient love with which he fulfilled his calling as we meet the demands of our own very different callings. We are therefore admonished by Paul (Phil. 2:5) to have "the mind of Christ" as we try to combine our God-given talents with our neighbor's needs.

For some this service will take the form of a public ministry of the word of God. It is essential for the life of a church that persons with the proper gifts be trained to lead congregations of Christians in their worship and witness. Most Christians, however, will continue to exercise their calling in domestic pursuits and public occupations. Most of the battles of life are fought by devoted Christian laypersons in their factories, marketplaces, kitchens, farms, and classrooms.

It follows that every believer engaged in socially useful work is called by God to full-time Christian service. The ordained ministry is simply one among many other functional offices of Christian service. Though only some Christians are called to serve the church as ordained pastors, all Christians are called to serve the world as baptized priests. As Luther put it most powerfully in his *Freedom of a Christian Man*, "I will give myself as a Christ to my neighbor, just as Christ offered himself to me."

Having rejected the late medieval church's double standard of clergymen with vocations and laypersons with none, Luther had two clear alternatives before him in the sixteenth century. He could say, strictly speaking, that *no* earthly occupation should be equated with one's heavenly vocation. Or he could carry through Paul's partial breakthrough in 1 Corinthians 7 (marriage, slavery, circumcision) to include *all* stations and occupations, lay as well as clerical, within the Christian's total stewardship of life under God.

Fortunately, Luther chose the second alternative. He insisted that God does not call you to *do* something but rather to *be* something, a Christian servant. Every person has an economic occupation, but the Christian views it as part of his/her religious vocation. There are no "sacred" callings over against "secular" callings. All of life is sacred when lived to the glory of God and the benefit of our neighbors.

This liberating message turns monastic theory upside down. It declares that the world is not here to serve the church, but rather that the church is here—like its Lord—to serve the world. If "God so loved the world that he gave his only Son" to serve in it and die for it (John 3:16), how dare his disciples attempt to isolate themselves from the challenges of life in some kind of pseudosanctity!

All discipleship worthy of the name "Christian" must begin reverently at the altar and end relevantly at the marketplace. The risen Christ with whom we live in the church is also the crucified Christ with whom we die in the world. The most crucial question is not, what are laypersons doing *in* the church? It is rather, what are they doing *as* the church in the world? The "ministry of the laity" expresses the privilege of the whole people of God to share in the mission of Christ's church. In return, laypersons have a right to expect their pastors to "equip the saints for the work of ministry . . . with the whole armor of God" (Eph. 4:12).

The Reformation thus included an ethical revolution within its "theology of the cross"—a cross situated originally not between two gold candlesticks on white linen but between two guilty criminals just outside the Jerusalem garbage dump. The church is truly the church when it looks and acts like the body of a crucified Head. It is deep in the midst of life that the Suffering Servant of God calls us to take up our cross and follow him in loving discipleship.


## ALL CHRISTIANS ARE PROPHETS

Regardless of the theology, however, it must be admitted at once that the social-ethical record of the Lutheran church leaves much to be desired. Despite a great deal of fine institutional work, this church has earned the reputation of being too apathetic in fighting for political and economic justice in society.

Lutheranism has tended to say that the church should "preach the gospel and administer the sacraments" and strictly limit its social witness to the daily lives of the laity. This concentration on the gospel has led to a soundly evangelical *personal ethic*: "faith active in love." But the whole vast realm of corporate structures and institutional life has often been deprived of the judgment and guidance of God's law by the church's neglect of any corresponding *social ethic*: "love seeking justice." Lutherans have traditionally been much stronger on the personal appropriation of the gospel than on the social demands of the law. But just as the gospel comforts the afflicted, so the law conflicts the comfortable. What we desperately need today is the addition of a prophetic counterpart to the church's universal priesthood. "Upon your walls, O Jerusalem, I have set watchmen; all the day and all the night they shall never be silent" (Isa. 62:6).

The rapid growth of an industrial way of life in post-Reformation Europe and America enabled ruthless persons to distort Luther's doctrine of vocation in three ways. Domestically, it sanctioned a patriarchal rule of family life by the father "called" by God for such discipline. Politically, it was often given a reactionary twist by providing church support for any ruler, whether just or not, who was "called" by God to bear the sword. Economically, it tended to baptize the "rugged individualism" of Protestant businessmen who allegedly could demonstrate God's blessing of their "calling" by the accumulation of vast economic power and possessions.

The Calvinist Reformation intensified the understanding of vocation as referring both to one's salvation and to God's call to express that salvation by glorifying him in the totality of one's life in the world. It was Puritan preachers on the Continent, in Great Britain, and later in the newly developing colonies who, more radically than Calvin himself, gave great emphasis in their sermons and writings to the relation of daily work and vocation. Work was a religious duty. It was to engross most of a person's time. Idleness and excessive merriment were eschewed as sinful. Through efforts of these preachers, the so-called "Protestant work ethic" became widely shared, and negative views of some forms of nonwork or leisure pursuits were given credence.[1]

In passing, it is also important to recall with Jackson W. Carroll that the time at which this virtual identification of one's calling by God and one's daily work was made was during the Industrial Revolution and later at the time of the settlement of the Americas. New jobs and new working conditions were coming into existence, breaking up time-honored patterns of life and work. There was need to motivate workers to accept the new patterns.

Also, often for survival sake, there was little room for idleness. Work had become a crucial issue, and the Puritan preachers attempted to interpret its religious significance to meet the new situation. Many of them went so far in making the identification of vocation and occupation that they lost any critical perspective from which to question both the idolatrous worship of work and success, and unjust and inhumane labor practices and business dealings.

A final development in the evolution of the idea of vocation was the almost complete loss of its religious significance. For most people, to speak of one's vocation gradually became synonymous with speaking of one's work or occupation. "Vocational training schools" began to prepare for a variety of jobs. There was no longer any religious significance implied. With this secularized degeneration, the so-called "Protestant work ethic" remained neither Protestant nor ethical.

The net effect was a conservative submission to the evils of the status quo. The righteous will of God was simply identified with existing forms of government and patterns of economic life. Obvious injustice was piously dismissed as part of the cross which had to be borne by Christian citizens and employees (but never rulers and employers)!

For example, economic justice was disregarded in favor of paternalism and philanthropy. It did not much matter how you made your money as long as you used some of your earnings to

1. For the most important discussion of this development, see Max Weber, *The Protestant Ethic and the Spirit of Capitalism*, trans. Talcott Parsons (New York: Charles Scribner's Sons, 1930).

support the institutional church and its otherworldly religion. Karl Marx was partly right in calling this kind of unbiblical faith an "opiate of the people." His proposed remedy in atheistic communism is a tragic reminder of how the world's sins of commission are often stimulated by the church's sins of omission.

A Protestant double standard has now arisen which is every bit as dangerous as the Roman Catholic form it replaced. Instead of separating the behavior of clergy and laity, we call all Christians "priests" but then divorce their religion from their job morality. What injustice the economic system demands of us is shrugged off as "Well, that's business." We put up with these evils on the job so we can have the time and resources to act as Christians in personal relations (off the job), at home, in church work, and in charitable activities.

God calls us to turn from sin and serve sinners in our work as well as our worship. But how, with endless miles of assembly lines and countless millions of workers throughout the world dependent upon every fluctuation in the New York Stock Exchange?

## THE CHRISTIAN'S ECONOMIC ETHIC

Obviously there is no "Christian" economy which we could dictate to the world as a magic solution. As a matter of fact we should reject any such "canon law" as a denial of both Christian and political freedom. The official pronouncements of the church on urgent social issues do not compel anything of anyone. Instead, they are designed to provide men and women with the faith and facts necessary to reach their own decisions for Christian social action.

This responsible freedom is championed by the church because the Bible is concerned with economic life only insofar as it aids or hinders our relation to God and other persons. Holy Scripture is not an economic textbook with pat answers to technical problems. There is no "Christian" economics, any more than there is Christian chemistry or plumbing. Nevertheless, there must be Christians who as economists, managers, and laborers view the economic facts of life from the perspective of the word of God.

This orientation begins with the confession that all life belongs to God who is its Creator and Preserver. He is the world's only absolute owner. "The earth is the Lord's and the fulness thereof" (Ps. 24:1). Were it not for his gracious gifts we would have nothing. Creator and creature must never be confused, and we creatures must recognize our God-given limits and responsibilities.

Created in the holy and loving image of God, we are stewards of his bounty. We are accountable for the ways in which we use, abuse, or neglect to use the manifold resources placed at our disposal. Reflecting God's cosmic dominion as Creator, we are called to "subdue the earth and have dominion [not "callously dominate"] every living thing" (Gen. 1:28). Our time, talents, and possessions are all temporarily loaned by God for our responsible care of others.

Private property, therefore, is never an absolute human right in Holy Scripture. As an aid to personal freedom it is a relative civil right that is always conditioned by the will of God and the needs of the community. The need to serve justifies the right to possess in God's created order of life-in-community. Nowhere does the Bible sanction the accumulation of economic power and possessions as ends in themselves. Then the almighty dollar ("mammon") replaces Almighty God.

Jesus Christ is God's answer to human sin. But the Son of God does not come as a social reformer with a new economic program. "Who made me a judge or divider over you?" (Luke 12:14), he asks the man who wants cheap economic advice.

We completely misinterpret the economic settings of many of the parables of Jesus if we forget that they are describing the kingdom of God, not prescribing the business of humans ("The kingdom of heaven is like . . ."). If any American company tried to enact the employment policy of the owner in the parable of the laborers in the vineyard (Matt. 20:1–16), Christians should be the first to put in a quick call to the National Labor Relations Board!

"Seek first his kingdom and his righteousness, and all these things shall be yours as well" (Matt. 6:33). It was not money as such but love of money that Christ condemned. It is not property as such that must be surrendered but the evil will that seeks in possessions a false idol. Ascetic poverty is never glorified by Christ. In fact, he was himself accused of being "a glutton and a drunkard" by some of the religious experts of his own day.

Christ's stress is always on purity of heart, our entry into the kingdom, our putting first things first. "For where your treasure is, there will your heart be also" (Matt. 6:21). Wealth is dangerous because of what it does to proud persons. We easily mix up what we have with what we are. We consistently forget that "a man's life does not consist in the abundance of his possessions" (Luke 12:15).

We covet the things of this world, "where moth and rust consume, and where thieves break in and steal" (Matt. 6:19). This does not mean that the poor are automatically more virtuous and less selfish than the rich. It means rather that it is the "poor in spirit" (whatever their economic status) who are given the kingdom of heaven. While God is no "respecter of persons" (Rom. 2:11), however, the Scriptures also make clear that the mission of God's people on earth is to favor the aid and advocacy of the poor, the suffering, and the disinherited.

## THE CHRISTIAN'S STRUGGLE FOR
## ECONOMIC JUSTICE

Redeemed by the cross of the crucified and risen Lord, Christians try to put these teachings into practice. While we do not have any blueprint for Utopia, there are at least three biblical insights that could help us in our ongoing search for more economic justice.

In the first place, we should destroy the false image of "mammon" which is still held by so many Christians. If God has created us with a diversity of gifts which we are to share with one another in personal and economic interdependence, then we must get it out of our heads that business is inherently "dirty."

It is not God's will that Christians flee from the economic order. Capital, nuclear energy, computers, and automation can all become false gods which deny the universal lordship of God.

But these economic instruments can also be employed by women and men of integrity for the benefit of all God's needy children.

Think of all the good that has been worked through the secular miracles of mass production in our modern mixed economy. Is it not ethically significant that dictators are defeated, the starving fed, epidemics checked, and millions of persons living above survival level for the first time in history? Our Christian answer to mammon is not retreat but reform.

In the second place, we Christians must learn to translate our personal love into economic justice. Justice is the form which love takes in meeting social inequities. Christians are at once both conservative and radical. As creatures in the old age of Adam, we serve wherever we are; as saints in the new age of Christ, we reform whatever we can.

We often fall into despair because we do not see the sacrificial love of Christ operative in business life. We must remember that this kind of love is possible only for perfect persons in personal relationships. However, business is run by imperfect people in mass relations. If we cannot even manage our little homes and congregations by the Sermon on the Mount, certainly we should not demand the impossible of giant corporations and labor unions.

Still, we have a right to expect far more than flagrant injustice in economic life. By virtue of the law of God written on the hearts of all his creatures, the justice of giving "each person his due" is generally recognized. Yet our economy has a much better record on mass production than on equitable distribution. The motto "The business of America is business" is more than callous economics; it is theological heresy.

This struggle for economic justice has now taken the form of massive power structures competing against each other in a dynamic system of checks and balances. Big machinery has brought big business; big business has been challenged by big labor; both are held accountable by big government. The old abuses of individualism have now been replaced by new threats of collectivism from all three directions.

Only through our active participation in all three power

structures as workers, union members, and citizens can we put teeth into our Christian social responsibility. Our economic have-nots would need a lot less remedial charity if they enjoyed a little more preventive justice. We must therefore keep the economic order subject to God both by serving it in love as his priests and by judging it in justice as his prophets. When we speak and act, the church is speaking and acting in praise of God. We are the church at work on the economic frontiers of life.

Finally, as Christians we engage in the economic order with a realism that saves us from both idealism and cynicism. We do not expect sinful men and women to transform our nation's economy into the kingdom of God. Nevertheless, we who are armed with the pardon and power of God can still testify to our Lord by helping to make justice more loving and efficiency more humane.

Let us be realistic. The demands of some jobs in our economy are so personally degrading and morally harmful that Christians had better leave them and be willing to take the consequences. We do not live by bread alone. Sometimes, for Christ's sake, a line simply has to be drawn. "For what will it profit a man, if he gains the whole world and forfeits his life?" (Mark 8:36).

Most times, however, we operate in morally gray areas. In varying degrees, our work both strengthens and weakens the general welfare of the community. Both virtues and vices are demanded; service is offered but corners are also cut. Christ called us to be both "wise as serpents and innocent as doves" (Matt. 10:16). How do Christian workers respond when the moral issues are not drawn clearly in black and white?

Here we will stick it out and fight alongside others to make things better. Many battles will be lost but a few will be won. Usually we will have to settle for half a loaf as better than nothing at all. We will find ourselves thrown together with some strange bedfellows, and we will be forced to make many prudential decisions and even tactical compromises. In short, clean hands are often impossible in a dirty world. Yet sins of omission are not inherently superior to sins of commission. This is what Luther meant by advising, "Sin boldly, but believe and rejoice in Christ even more boldly!"

Our ethical "solutions" to the economic dilemmas of life remain so religiously ambiguous that Christians must put their ultimate trust in God's mercy alone. After all is said and done, Jesus Christ provides our only saving righteousness before God. It is therefore not moral perfection but religious forgiveness which is the church's last word to God's responsible stewards.

# Whatever Happened to the "Protestant Ethic"?

WHEN discussing contemporary economic problems in a church basement with sincere and devoted Christian men and women, I am frequently confronted by a well-dressed gentleman who clinches the argument against Aid to Dependent Children or some other project offensive to him by saying, "As the Bible says, 'God helps those who help themselves.'" If one has the temerity to wonder where the Bible makes this edifying observation, one is attacked as obviously ignorant of the most basic assertions of true Christian faith.

What has been loosely defined as "the Protestant ethic" has in ordinary discourse only remote similarity with the sophisticated theory developed first by Max Weber (1904) and modified by a library of learned studies since, but it is alive and well in church basements across the land. Besides asserting that God is on the side of the self-made man, it makes an economic dogma out of Jesus' offhand remark in defense of the woman who was anointing him with precious ointment and who offended Judas's acquisitive instincts. Because Jesus said "The poor you always have with you" (John 12:18), innumerable people have used this descriptive remark made two thousand years ago as an economic platform advocating the necessity and permanence of poverty.

Similarly, Paul's command in 2 Thessalonians 3:10, "If any one will not work, let him not eat," has been taken out of its context. Paul was telling enthusiastic Christians to carry their own weight and not to live as idle busybodies while expecting the second coming of Christ. This saying has been used in a highly selective manner to oppose unemployment compensation and relief in the modern industrial society. Of course, someone who has not lifted a finger in a lifetime because of inherited wealth is not considered as falling under Paul's condemnation. The poor who do not work, even if they have been vainly looking for work, are clearly more offensive to this "bowdlerized" version of the Protestant ethic than the rich who do not work.

All this would not be very interesting if it did not reveal a dangerous heresy. Modern Christians, especially in the industrialized, so-called developed countries, may not believe in salvation by the good works which inspired hope and confidence in their medieval ancestors. They put little trust in conventional good works like almsgiving. They may diet but certainly do not fast. Obedience or chastity are not much stressed. These are all considered "bad" good works. It is commonly believed that salvation is the same as success competitively achieved, preferably in business or the professions. The sign of God's good pleasure may once have seemed clanking chains, hairshirts, and even bloody stigmata on hands, feet, and in the side of the body. Today they are powerboats, motor homes and semiannual "cruises."

But how about the young? An attractive and intelligent young woman, a freshman in one of my discussion groups, told us the other day that she had come to college for two reasons—to become rich and to become famous. And nobody laughed or wept. A decade after the student revolt, the greening of America, and Consciousness Three, the "Protestant ethic" is doing well. It may not be Protestant or much of an ethic, but it is doing very well.

G.W.F.

# The Clergy Crisis

Anyone who has talked to ordained ministers in recent years must be aware of the fact that as a profession the clergy are going through a severe crisis. The reasons for their obvious and pervasive uncertainty are numerous. Some are clearly economic. In a period of rapid inflation the clergy are always trying to catch up—and falling further and further behind. Some subsist at a poverty level, which creates problems in a society where worth is measured in money. In those terms the average pastor isn't "worth" very much.

If Protestants at least would make this poverty an "evangelical counsel" bringing one closer to God, it would not be so bad. But it is apparent that "successful" Protestant clergy are also well-paid clergy. Inflation has thus undermined the sense of professional accomplishment for many. To be specific and somewhat anecdotal: if I compare the 1968 college graduate who is now in his second parish with the equally intelligent college graduate now working for a major law firm or practicing a medical specialty, it is quite possible that the lawyer may be earning three times as much and the physician five times as much as the equally hard-working pastor. While I have not made a statistical survey, I have former students, personal friends, of whom this is true. They are all good people who do their respective jobs in a competent and dedicated fashion. The physician, a woman, earns more than the other two combined.

While finances are certainly a factor in the present malaise, they are not the only factor. A second reason for the uncertainty is the fact that the pastor is the last generalist in an age of specialists. Ministers are supposed to be so many things to so many people that they often feel that they mean nothing to anybody. The lawyer who is asked a legal question he cannot answer can always say, "That is not my field." The dermatologist can always say, "I am not an obstetrician." What does the pastor say? She or he is supposed to be a competent business manager, youth director, psychologist, social worker, speech writer, orator, and theologian, to mention only a few of the essential qualifications. No wonder angst has become the pastor's middle name.

In addition, there is a surplus of clergy and of candidates in seminaries in most Protestant denominations. Those pastors who are unhappy in their present locations know that they are probably stuck; the surplus of clergy has reduced their mobility.

There may be other reasons. I would hazard a guess that the self-understanding of so many theological seminaries as graduate

261.85

F715

64952

schools in religious studies or the philosophy of religion has not helped very much. Medical schools never thought they were merely graduate schools in biochemistry or physiology.

Whatever the reasons, the mood is apparent everywhere. Solutions will have to be found, and some will meet with fierce resistance. As a discussion-starter, I would like to suggest that we take the functional character of the ordained ministry seriously. Men and women should not feel trapped in the clergy because of some notion that they would betray God if they did something else to earn a living. Ordination as an "indelible character" is so deeply rooted in the self-image of the clergy that it sometimes obscures obvious alternatives to an impossible situation.

Another possibility is the ordained ministry as a part-time profession. The much-maligned "tentmaking ministry" deserves further exploration and evaluation. In order to make it work, the institutional churches would have to relate to the "tentmakers" in a much more direct and meaningful manner.

Last but not least, the problem should not be left to the clergy alone to worry about. It is a serious concern for the entire people of God. We are all affected by it and should all work toward a solution.

G.W.F.